CALL THIS ROOM A STATION

CALL THIS ROOM A STATION

poems

John Willson

MoonPath Press

Poetry
ISBN 978-1-936657-45-2

Cover art by Patty Rogers
We Keep It Inside Us, 2015
72 x 36 inches
acrylic, conté, collage on canvas

Author photo by Luciano Marano

Book design by Tonya Namura,
using Gill Sans and Minion Pro.

MoonPath Press is dedicated to publishing the finest poets living in the U.S. Pacific Northwest

MoonPath Press
PO Box 445
Tillamook, OR 97141

MoonPathPress@gmail.com

http://MoonPathPress.com

to Kim

I require a You to become;
becoming I, I say You.

~Martin Buber

Contents

CALL THIS ROOM A STATION

I

Morning

There, again, piercing the chatter of other birds,
a long, single whistle, like a referee's whistle
stopping play, the bird itself hidden by salal
and the shadows of madrona and fir. An arrow
of sound shoots me back to an alpine dawn: sunlight

through tent fabric turned my hands
blue as the water where I swam until my eyes
opened to the same whistle. Creature that stays
from sight, how do you range from a mountain
down to this sea-level hawking
of crows, the finches' gossip?
Again, your pure syllable

taut as a tent line from apex to ground.
Did you see the flap open, watch me crawl
out, scoop water to my face,
scratch my chin when glasses
turned a white blob into a goat
above the pass? First-Thing-in-the-Morning,
I have never seen the color of your soft
throat, but with a wingbeat's ease

you shuttle me across the distance, pump
thin air into my lungs, turn me
toward the dwarf lupine by my boot.
Though you remain anonymous as a painter
of ancient caves, I salute you with a cup of tea
and I would welcome your call as the signal,
the last sound before my leaving the flesh, the whistle
bearing me into the wild blue.

The Wedded Rocks

Iséshima

A band of rippled light
cuts beneath a rope suspended
between them. More like mother and son,
these islands, the pointed one on the left like a mountain
tip, the smaller one squared off, but inclined
toward the other, as if moored by the trunk-
thick rope looped around the tops, its arc resting

like a hammock or a spider web's
strand heavy with dew. The rope bridges
sunrise, steel-blue ocean and orange sky,
the rocks one to another like words or days
or generations, and somewhere a man shoulders
bundled rice across a wooden bridge.

Standing here ages ago, a person
might have seen a goddess, a gate,
uncoiled a gesture to make it so,
climbing the rocks in turn. Photographs,
prayers, coins for the wooden offering box,
the buses come and go and the sun
turns the rope from silhouette

to hemp, cotton tassels hanging
in five bunches. Something remains I cannot
see or pronounce, something like the tide's
pull and flow, a ceremony joining
the reason I come to a place
and the reason I leave.

Departure

Japan 1936 / U.S. 2008 / U.S. 1968

I

Yen in hand, twenty-three years old, you lean
out your coach window—the vendor takes notice,
the tray that rides his waist
supported by a strap across his shoulders.

* * *

The teapot rests on my desk, empty,
glazed and square, you having found
the purchase worthy of keeping. Its cup,
turned upside down, serves
also as a lid.

2

Father, I call this room a station, memory
a platform, conjure your departure, you
at fifty-four—the age I turn today—
I at thirteen: late for junior high,

I rush into your bedroom.
A doctor stands beside where you lie.
I dig through Mom's purse for lunch money.
Where are your manners? you ask, irritation
in your last words to me.

3

The vendor steps back.
Inside the coach, ceramic warms your palm.
You pour a cup from a spout
whose curve bears

grace for both of us.
I exhale with your train as it eases
out of Gifu—rhymes with *me
too*—the stop you will pencil
on the teapot's unglazed base.

Garden Without Figures

China, 1936

Four or five steps away from the circular
entrance through a white wall
you focus on the rock-bound pond inside.
Softened in the foreground
interlocking Ts and Ls in the carved mahogany gate
and glossy tiles that rim the opening

occupy the width of your field.
Replacing the lens cap
you accept the wisteria's
blossoming invitation of shade
                    under a bamboo trellis—

you step across the threshold to a cobbled path
that curves into a garden
leaving me
this framed view on my desk
my face reflected in the glass
                  my eyes your eyes.
You leave me quietly   Father

the way you always moved
the way you left when I was thirteen:
you in bed with a nagging chest cold one day
absent the next day after school
never coming home from the hospital.
You left me angry at your calm

precision—the perfect
drop of glue at the tip of your toothpick
the day we joined the engine block
halves of the Model T we built—
you built—seamless

and intricate as a Chinese garden
the day I only wanted to play outside.
You left me angry at your weak heart

and the rest of my life without you
but here with you
outside a garden where I've never been—
a garden I remember for you—
I find a stillness.

Oban Entry

The horse would every so often stick his head
over my shoulder as if to read along,
but I knew he wanted more caramels,
nibbling at my coat. It was the chapter where Bilbo
finds the magic ring and tricks Gollum

in the Misty Mountains, and the mountains
dropped down to Loch Linnhe where I sat
by a pasture fence, hitchhiking between the Skye
ferry and Oban when I was twenty.
Hours later, perched on castle ruins,

I would enter Bilbo and the horse
in this diary. If my hitchhiking self
had seen me today on the same road,
straining to hold the rental car to the left—
if the two days had somehow merged and I

had pulled over by the pasture to offer
myself a ride—would he have seen
his future under thinning hair?
I leave him his book and caramels,
enter Oban for the second time,

creeping in first gear, in the trail
of tour bus fumes. My luggage lost
between Seattle and Glasgow, I glance
at each storefront, searching
for a shop that sells briefs.

Figuring the Landscape

The distant waterfall is a brush stroke
like green tea pouring from a spout.
Leaning on crutches, he spots a path.
It switchbacks through pines,
vanishes in mist at the click
of the museum guard's shoes.
He inches his cast forward,

the fractured ankle, recalls boots,
backpack, a clearing near tree line, a faint
roar across the valley—a cascade
tracing a fault down granite.
Will I ever go there again?
he asks himself, replies *Stupid, stupid,*
for the ankle cracked on his own slick deck

as he turned from looking at the stars.
Above mist, the path reaches a bamboo hut
and two seated figures with cups of tea
on the last of six folded panels.
He places himself there for a moment—
a sip, the time it takes the fibula to knit one
stitch—then turns his crutches away.

Repository

With patches the color of darkened blood
where lacquer has not worn off,
with carved folds of your gown hanging
vertically with cryptomeria grain, and a round
jewel embedded in your forehead,
you stand on a slate platform, above schoolchildren
chattering on their way to see the samurai swords.
Away from the incense and candle smoke

of the temple where you gave your own light,
you bear up under this arid climate,
illuminate a docent's passing comment:
Fine example of a twelfth-century Kannon.
Kannon—*The One Who Hears the Cries
of the World*—Goddess of Mercy,
it has come to this: you
stripped of the supplicant's prayer,

I with my admission ticket,
a sorrow that has no name.
Did the temple beams rot,
crack under moss and rain, did vines
grow across the altar?
Were you purchased for a song,
transported in the belly
of a B-29? I follow your left arm

down to the extended hand,
the upturned palm, the fingers poised
to gather in these heart beats. Who is to say
if either of us is in the wrong place?
We are what we are: you,

carved, wood ears with pendulous lobes,
and I, leaving you to the centuries,
stepping toward the next room.

Blacksmith

Philip Simmons, Charleston, South Carolina

Long fingers interlaced in your lap,
hands that steadied iron, swung
the hammer, you sit on a sofa, just shy
of ninety, master of gates, your cottage
a stop on the Gullah Tour.
When I speak of a stop on Wentworth,

the gates of your memory
swing: *Yes, a big white house,*
set back from the street.
By the sidewalk you measured the space
between white walls of the driveway,
envisioned your signature

scrolls balanced in the gate's halves,
spirals tight as those of whelk shells
across the harbor on Sullivan's Island,
the beach where your ancestors entered
this country as cargo of the Middle Passage.
If you see it curve like that, it's either

two hundred years old, or I done it,
you say of your scrolls, wrought one
above another, gracing the property line.
Centering your gate, parallel,
hammered ripples rise: twin paths
minnows might leave, startled upward.

To transplant

a flowering cherry, choose, if you are allowed
a choice, winter's dormancy over this
miserable time, this green April
afternoon when I severed roots
that fattened leaf and flower buds.
Start with a good reason—say,

that it grows where tomorrow a bulldozer
excavates—then find a spot of like drainage,
soil, knowing even there it arrives
an immigrant in foreign light. Prune
branches to the circumference of thirst
cut by your spade, prune as you would

leave behind all you own for the longest
journey this side of dying. When you dig
a root ball, hearing roots crack
like knuckles against your gentlest
leverings, don't stop to wonder how
a plant recoils, something beyond us even if,

months later, branches turn to sticks, leaves
curl and fall like ashes. After the last
root surrenders, bend to embrace
the ball, lift it from crater
to wheelbarrow. Walk the uneven
ground to the new hole, the tree

quivering like a landed fish.
Once you have placed it, backfilled,
and set a hose at the basin's uphill side,
take your shovel by the blade, poke
the handle around the perimeter, feeling out
air pockets, making mud of everything

roots touch. It is here that you pause
and say, or do not say, a few words, promise
weekly waterings, cross your heart and hope
for rain—anything but this muttered,
thick-tongued apology, the hose
a question mark in the grass.

Love Notes

Huachuca Mountains, Arizona

I

W.H. Frierson—1855-1928—
lies here, his mining pick's
iron head centered
at the foot of his tombstone, creekside,
just off the trail. Those dates,
he could have heard Geronimo in the snap

of a twig. Lovers of rust, we wander
his cabin's remains: scattered planks
pointing toward a porch, a banjo song.
We water up, having almost
played out this vein.

2

Potent in blue air
just across the saddle between canyons,
nine-foot stalk of agave
rises. Thick as a thigh, it strains
to burst into flower. Beside its base
of spiked flaring leaves we sway,
sweat-soaked, shadowless.

3

They dart and swoop
high above the crag where we sit
with Jarlsberg and apples, white-throated swifts,
six or seven of them, tails forked. One
dives toward another and they fuse. The tiny

mass plummets into the canyon. Half a breath
from the creek bed below us
they fly apart.

Back door towhee

scared in from the feeder,
your tiny panicked breaths
fog the glass, your beak flared, halting

on the sill between thrusts at the impossible
green outside.
Your heart must explode

when you dodge my towel-wrapped hands,
and a frayed charcoal feather
with a notch of white at the tip

rests on the floor by the television.
Again you lunge toward the photinia bush,
the sight of home turned inside out.

Look, I dumbly
tell you, *I'm late for work.*
Now, your breath my breath, I'm quick

enough to gather you away from the pane,
and on the porch, you shoot
out of my hands.

You call with a dead sea lion

to John Davis

four feet long on your beach, and concerned
about the backyard funeral tomorrow for the dowager
next door, neighbors have noted the stench. No state
agency will touch it, tides won't bear it
away. Rubber gloved you tried rolling it, found

what gravity lives in sloughing flesh
and thought of a shroud made of netting, towed
out to the channel, anchored with cinder blocks.
Wondering how a broad black nose, flared
whiskers and fins decompose, I can't tell you
where to find the material, whether one
buys it by the yard—I've never
been in the market—but

wait: in our garage is a hammock
we haven't strung for three houses, wanting
the right pair of trees. Take it, friend. Cinch it
until brown fur stands out in rectangles.
And may your boat's engine catch at the cord's
first pull, may the weight sink
swiftly on release, and may we all
sleep tight. I'll leave it on the driveway.

Eagle, Border Waters

Near Neah Bay, Strait of Juan de Fuca

Binoculars resolve what looked like a white
chunk of Styrofoam—your head.
In a mire of kelp about a hundred
fifty yards out, you flap, bob,
chitter to four eagles who circle,
dive toward you,

chitter back, fly off west.
This is near the end comes my mother's
voice on the phone yesterday,
ninety-four, hounded by a kidney infection.
We are alone in this world.
You zero in on the nearest

spot of beach, where I stand.
Your wing-splashes take on rhythm,
fusing butterfly, breast stroke,
Vancouver Island behind you.
Should you even reach the shore,
exhausted, I envision the ease

a coyote might enjoy,
a mass of soaked feathers on sand.
Your swim has taken you more than halfway
to where I pose a greater threat.
I turn, step into wind
that blows down the mouth of the Strait.

Urgent buzzing at my feet

draws me down to inspect you
dragonfly with one pair of net-veined
wings stuck in mud by the swamp's edge

the other pair beating for the sky
your faceted eyes rotating
wildly independent of each other

black ants running up your body
that the Japanese named a pencil after—
tombow—you looking for all

the world fallen
like bamboo bent   not broken.
Well here we are

alive but bound
in need of a miracle   even such a miracle
as I could deliver by

throwing you out to the water
for the mercy of a bird or a fish.
And so I take your wings

between my fingers
lift you out of the mud
fling you into the air where you

hover for a moment
shaking out a rainbow
among a host of your fellows

before you dart away
                    leaving me
no angels but in dragonflies.

Mother's Day at Ninety-three

*I tried to miscarry you by jumping
up and down*, you tell me over toast
and marmalade, aluminum walker
parked by your chair, your Boston terrier
snarfing crumbs blindly underfoot.
Did you look like me when I'm poolside,
jumping to shake water from my ear?

Cambria—"where pines meet the sea"—
a retreat for you and Dad, your last
child seven years old.
Your diaphragm stared from the bedside
table at the moon, and I was out of the blocks.
*I had four already, and really
didn't think I could cope with another.*

I remember us in a life raft, our last
family trip, you, Dad and me, water
thick with oil, kelp.
Our ferryboat lay up on stone
that had ground us awake through the cabin floor.
Later I wore sneakers and a blanket
Kwakiutl people gave me.
Wait here with your father—at the tribal
pharmacy I sat while Dad got his tiny
white pills: nitroglycerine.
Refugees, we all watched an Eagle Dance
in a longhouse, a gift from our
short-notice hosts in Alert Bay.

You stood behind me, sheet
safety-pinned around my neck, me squirming
on the stool till you screamed
I won't take this anymore,
hurled the scissors.
Steel quivered in the pantry door—
one loop and its finger rest formed
a hanging letter Q.
Would you have jumped higher
to miscarry, had you known Dad,
the family barber, would die
that year, the year I would turn thirteen?

My wife pours your second cup of tea.
Breast cancer followed her miscarriage—
what was to have been our first child.
High-dose chemo stilled her womb.
I place the sugar bowl on your right—
Thank you, dear.
We called you "our dividend."
Don't forget that.

This morning, after helping you dress, I pulled
white hair from your brush, a mat
the size of a quarter, so fine and soft
I tucked it into my wallet.

Epithalamium

Mother never fails to find
                        a four-leaf clover.
She will step out of the car
                        bend over the parking strip
brush her foot across a patch of green:

There's one, see?
            Here. Take it.
                 Take it.

She always gives them
                   and we press them into books
so that reading some day
                 we turn a page
and the gift of a four-leaf clover
                     falls into our lap.

As children we spent hours
                   trying to find four-leaf clovers
staining our knees green
                 asking each other
How does she do it?

Grown now, I still ask:
How *does* the eye spot four
                 in an ocean of threes?

How *do* you find love?

Four-leaf clovers are still
                 difficult to find

but I think I have learned
            that we cannot separate
the finding eye
            from the giving heart.

We search.
    We find.
        We give—

we say, *Here. Take it.*
            Take it.

So you search and search.

It takes a long time
            but you know it's there—

it takes your whole life
                but it's there, it's there
in all the places you have been

all the places you will go

and here, as you look
            into each other's eyes

seeing in those eyes
            what others do not see

finding there
        what others cannot find

and giving: *Here. Take it.*
                Take it.

The Order of Things

Cooper's Barbecue, Llano, Texas

His turn to face the Pit Man,
head of a line that snakes outside,
the parking lot thronged on a Saturday.
His mother pulls her eighty-eight years
out of the rental's back seat.
Mesquite smoke rises from pits of steel
that resemble oil barrels laid open,
and his mother walks, the woman who griddled
Sunday burgers, taught him
to suck the marrow from a lamb bone.
He points to a spot on a brisket of beef
when the Pit Man's blade asks *where*.
His mother's forearm catches
the edge of the side view mirror,
flesh peels back in a three-inch crescent,
tissue white beneath.
He feels the wound in his own
forearm, reaches for his pocket
handkerchief as the Pit Man cleaves
the brisket in one stroke.

Grace Below the Pass

Olympic Mountains, Washington

In the dirt between us lie splayed
noodles, the aluminum pot my hand flicked.

Larkspur at the foot of the trail, asters, lupine,
Indian paintbrush on the scree slope

mid-afternoon—all vanish in a wash of dismay.
Bury them, eat crackers

I think, but you instruct us both to gather
them—grit, fir needles and all—

back into the pot,
carry them to the spring.

We lower strands just shy of *al dente*—
they flow in bundles

between our fingers
through the purest waters we've known.

We lose not a single one.
On propane's hiss again, the pot

climbs to a boil, bearing
a resurrected appetite

for smoked salmon pesto,
spring-rinsed angel hair.

Anthropomorphic

Kalaloch, Washington

We walked on sand marbled by clouds
like smoke on a skin of water. Or a cloud-
plate, breaking up as it slid eastward, opening
a horizon blue as the tide was low. Salt wind,

drift logs a banked high water mark,
salal and scrub spruce—even these left
bits of last night's quarrel unscoured
from our minds. Who should have done the dishes!
Oh how we polished the art of ending

in separate rooms. In connecting rooms—you
with a mystery novel on the sofa, I in the kitchen
window nook—we pilot the rented cabin. Below
the bluff, a creek stretches from the forest,

splitting the beach into loins, driftwood
on either side a tangle of hair.
Close your mystery. At this delta where
salt and fresh waters mix in whirlpools, the salt
water rising to meet the fresh, the fresh water

a tongue sucked by the moon—here
let us lie on the musty mattress, penetrate
the incoming tide all the way
through sunset, slip down a flood of silk
to make dishwater seem coarse.

2

The Motorist's Prayer

I could take that priest for an ancient poet
with his white moustache and pointed beard
but he wears a tall black hat and Shinto robes
chanting beside a brand new
Mitsubishi sedan with all four doors open
while a young couple stands aside

respectful in their Sunday best.
In both hands he holds a bamboo wand
with long paper tassels
waves it three times above the driver's seat
stiffly walks to the open hood
                              passes white tassels
three times across the engine at this shrine

on the Old Tokaido Road.
Prayermobile—that's the name my friends
gave the '63 Plymouth Belvedere four-door
Parson Pearson blessed me with when he
bought his new Ford

and I was sixteen.
The Prayer for short—
            my first car—
eight years off the assembly line
always started eagerly and settled
into neutral with a hum and a quiet
ticking like a watch.
Space Age push-buttons

in a vertical row left of the steering column
shifted me smoothly into lurching adolescence
and I did my best to ignore the chrome
sticker on the ash tray door

bearing The Motorist's Prayer:
Oh Lord keep my hands
                          steady upon the wheel.
Forbid that my carelessness should . . .
How does the rest of it go?
My carelessness should have

turned every intersection into a collision
the times when hot blood fueled me
but something more than luck or my godless
prayers behind the wheel—some steadiness
living in the car itself—
willed me between the white lines and always
got me home. In the driver's seat

any destination became a home
like the cliffs where I parked and sunset
darkened the sky to rust on the ocean.
That car was made for eternity
said Parson Pearson as I stepped out of The Prayer
years later at his home in another town.
I slipped the key from the ignition for the last time

to live in this country where a priest
waves a bamboo wand over the trunk of a car.
Where is The Prayer now?
Breakdown makes life

a journey to the junkyard
but that machine moved me
and here on this old
cobbled highway between ancient
and modern capitals
I send it this blessing—
                          a distant benediction
long after my hands left the wheel.

Pilothouse, the *Hoy Lass*

Inner Hebrides, Scotland

You slow the engines upon entering
Loch Tuath—*Toó-uh*—pronounce
your native Gaelic in the passage
between the isles of Mull and Ulva,
the Gaelic for which you received

abuse as a schoolboy.
Earlier, puffins by the hundreds
flew from the sea to their cliffside burrows
and cameras clicked their daily return.
An inquisitive melancholy

streaked from two corners
of the birds' triangular eye markings,
black across their white faces.
The tour nearing its end, you gesture south
to Ulva, a wide beach, a row of stone

cottages in ruins. *Starvation Point,*
you tell me, off the public address.
People thrown out
of their homes during the Clearances
lived there until boats

carried them and their Gaelic to America
or Nova Scotia or elsewhere. Elsewhere—
somewhere other than home—a place
for which no speakable word
exists, in Gaelic or in English,

when home is your thatched roof torched,
your fields given over to sheep.
You ease the boat alongside the dock,
landing us, returning us to Mull,
your home and nowhere else.

Roommates

With a snore to rival a truck
Jake braking, Gloria, the caregiver,
reposed on the fold-out couch to my left.
Spine twisting into the recliner, I wrestled

blankets and a pillow given by the nurse.
Mom, having seniority, occupied
the bed, wall-mounted boxes dispensing
her diet: oxygen tubing to her nose,
morphine to envelop the canyon

of the bedsore by her coccyx.
I slept or did not sleep
four nights to stereo: the diesel
gears propelling Gloria's dreams, the rattle

that marked Mom's breathing.
Mom lay unspeaking, save the night
she cried, *Help, I'm falling! Hold my arms!*
Startled to her side,
I stroked Mom's hand,

pressed a cool cloth to her forehead.
Que lucha! I whispered across
her breathing form.
Bastante lucha, Gloria whispered back.

Enough fight.
In the recliner again, eyes closed,
I counted Mom's exhalations—
white volleyballs—lofted each
back over the net.

Slow Starter

Reaching for the last of my wind,
I hear the horn blast—one
more minute—the bulk of my years
four blocks from the boat. Father, I fail,

as I chug through the drizzle, to make
myself back into the quarter miler
who flew like a feather in high school,
whose chest broke the tape. But I see you,
whose heart ran out of time when I
entered my teens—I see you at your jigsaw,

cutting me a plywood discus.
We drove your Bug to the deserted track.
With stopwatch and measuring tape you gave me
a shot at everything: hurdles, high jump,
standing and running long jump.
At the starting line you dug foot holes
with a trowel, as you did in the days

before blocks. All bony legs and sneakers,
I felt the strangeness of sprinting a fifty against
myself. You wrote times and distances in a notebook
carried in your shirt pocket with your pills.
Since you passed me your genes like a baton,

how can I complain that you never saw
me in spikes and team colors? Yes,
you, the first state high schooler to break
ten seconds in the hundred. Though you
didn't stick around for just one meet,
we both, at different times but stride
for stride, checked our lanes for loose dirt, smelled
adrenaline in the field's cut grass.

Crouched at our marks, our heads hung
at the apex of an isosceles triangle.
Today it is enough to be the ragged
last passenger on a late ferry pulling away,
the horn blast filling my nostrils
like smoke from the starting pistol.

Combination, 1968

Master® out of Milwaukee with a rusty
bolt, unearthed
while clearing the garage,
it hung on my wooden
locker, junior high.
What anchors this morning—what rests

in my palm—trembled
as I turned the knob right
to seven on the first
day back after my father died.
Turning left past seven to twenty-nine,
I wondered, of the kids

streaming behind me,
who knew, as though to lose
a father were a shame.
Right, on the way
to thirty-five, I saw
the locker as a standing coffin,

though he was cremated, wasn't he,
and the locker door had a row of drilled
holes at the bottom.
My English binder, *Más Practica,*
The Count of Monte Cristo,
texts I had left

to go home and find him not there
awaited the tumblers'
release. Now the bolt slides open.
Not crying may have been like
snapping it shut, with a turn
to make sure it stayed locked.

Pages from a Wall Calendar

"Snail, snail, glister me forward…"
Theodore Roethke, *The Lost Son*

November is a snail on bamboo.
Between two of the stem's held breaths,
the ridge on the joint has diverted the snail's
upward progress. The shell blazes, a spiral
yellow on green.

December is a stone that stands
among other stones, white gravel
raked in ripples around them. Stones
and white gravel, the Zen garden fills the pool
where the greenhouse poet died swimming.

Snow-slick roads of January having kept
me two weeks from swimming, I enter the pool
slowly, stretch my arms backward, minding
the rotator cuff. A year older
than my father when pneumonia

and a coronary took him, I push off, goggles
trained on the black line, the first lap underwater.
How would it feel, water flowing into these lungs?
I near the cross-mark at the deep end, rise,
coil, burst out of the turn.

Thirty-six Views of Mt. Fuji

to Hokusai

Ghost-cone

caught between skyscrapers
                    the morning after a typhoon

clipped by power poles
into segments from the bullet train window

or here in the background
                    focusing landscapes
you peopled with desire for travel:
viewed over the backs and upturned

bamboo hats of your figures:
an open ferry boat pulling out
                            across the Sumida
listing under its passengers

packhorse and palanquin
                    against a row of pines
on a lakeside highway

three men trying to join hands around
                            an old cryptomeria tree
at Mishima Pass   failing to encircle it
before continuing

on foot—the only way to know
                    every inch of the path
is the destination itself.

I live in an age of argument
over speed limits—
                    the scenery from one point
to the next so blurred

we never really get there—
but you were the master of travel-
                              without-arrival:
a lifetime of ninety-three homes

thirty-one pen names
                    the last name—
Old Man Mad With Painting—signing
the letter in which you enclosed
                         a self-portrait

supported by paint brushes
                   in place of crutches:
. . . as for my life
it is no longer in public view
and I cannot give you my address.

That bald man in print
                    after print
gazing up at the hub
                of your circular pilgrimage
his head like an egg

seen on end—
            the man at the tiller
of the ferry—Hokusai
                    is that you?

Miyajima, Boys Day

A vermilion *torii*—a seagate
with gull stains dripping down the cross beams—
measures low tide at the entrance to the bay.

Pines slope down
            from the island's mountain
to a vermilion shrine along the shore

a temple with rice paddles—votives
bearing handwritten prayers—bundled
                        and piled in back

silk carp
      one for each son
                  billowing over the houses

and a souvenir shop:
                  on this shelf
a carving from a pine limb where a smaller

limb branched off:
Daruma—Bodhidharma—
Zen patriarch resting in my palm

I darken your pendulous earlobes
                        with oil from my brow.
You would tell me how your legs atrophied

and fell away
how your eyelids distracted meditation
                        so you cut them off

and they became tea leaves
but wood grain spreads your face
                        into a mute grimace

and concentric rings
                describing the dome of your head
direct me over water and land

ten miles to Hiroshima
city of seven rivers that wind together
and enter the sea as one tongue.

Pine Islands: A Letter to Bashō

"Days and months are travelers of eternity.
So are the years that pass by."
The Narrow Road to the Deep North, 1691

You sold your house in Edo
thinking never to return
took the road north with a bamboo staff

brush and paper
the heaviest things in your bundle.

Caught by a storm
three days in a gatekeeper's house
you found occasion for haiku:

Bit by fleas and lice,
I spent the night, horse pissing
                              beside my pillow.

The road grew colder
                    and narrower
the frosted grass reminding you of your hair
as you held to your direction:

There are hundreds of crossroads on the moor
a farmer told you
and this horse knows the way.
Send him back when he will go no farther.

From Shiogama you hired a rowboat—
                              I followed

48

in a double-decker boat
                        shaped like a peacock
loudspeakers touting the natural wonders—
and we rounded the same peninsula

to the Bay of Matsushima
                        with its hundreds of islands
their bases eroded to the angle of bonsai trays
pines twisting over water.

Passing islands white from first snow
I remembered your haiku:

Ah Matsushima!
  Ah Matsushima ah ah!
                        Matsushima ah!

We both found an inn
                        overlooking the bay
and sat before open windows
                        as the islands darkened.

I wrote: "Jigsaw pieces
                        whose edges do not touch—no.

A maze with passages of water—no."

You wrote: *My pen strove in vain.*

The full moon rose
and boiled the rippling bay
                        into quicksilver
marked by the bamboo uprights of the oyster beds.

Uses of Bamboo

. . . from the Malay word
describing the explosions
of a grove on fire.

Ring-knuckles join
and divide sections
        each drawing a breath

underground and holding it
        in a black cylinder

until a knife splits
        light into strands:

(window screen) (flower basket) (lamp shade)
(comb) (tea whisk)

The smooth distance between joints

stands for virtue
        between faults

the hollow interior
        humility.

(water scoop) (cup) (chopsticks) (toothpick)
(pipe) (ink brush)

In the middle of winter
a dying mother asked
        for a bowl of soup

made from bamboo shoots.
Her son wept
        in the frozen grove:

shoots burst from
        the tear-softened ground.

(vaulting pole) (hiking staff) (stilts)
(crutch) (cane) (cradle)

At intervals of thirty
or even one hundred and twenty years

all plants
of a given species
        flower and die.

Seedlings may take ten
        years reaching maturity.

(sun hat) (water pipe) (scarecrow)
(rake) (drying rack) (sieve)

After trying thousands
of materials   Thomas Edison

found carbonized bamboo
        for the filament of his

electric light bulb.

(fence) (gate) (roof tile) (gutter)
(rain spout) (door frame)

(concrete reinforcement) (skyscraper scaffolding)

Museum exhibit:
samples from a grove

flattened like blinds
           after a white
flash over Nagasaki.

Kannon

The one who hears the voices of the world.

Worshipped secretly as Mary by underground
Japanese Christians more than three hundred
years ago in Nagasaki.

I Hase Temple (Kamakura)

Kannon—god
        goddess of Mercy
carved from a thirty-foot
                cedar log—

gilt goddess with a flowing moustache

Kannon of children lost
        to miscarriage   disease
accident   abortion:

the father puts a small
        open cup of yogurt
on the altar

and the mother a plastic spoon
      whistle   red-and-blue pinwheel—

they clap hands twice
          toss coins
into the wooden box
         pray   clap twice.

By the temple gate
      at sunset: cats mating—
his teeth locked
      into her ruff.

Snow slides down
                the curved copper roof.

2 Setagaya Temple (Tokyo)

    In the courtyard
a priest wearing a white
            T-shirt prunes bonsai azalea.

Wind stirs cherry petals—
                a boy rushes
to catch them with his baseball cap.

Kannon-in-bronze stands
                    on koi-patrolled water
Kannon of the 4,650 Kamikaze.
        Inside: a photo

on the candlelit wall: young men
                        in leather helmets
arms raised in pre-flight *sake*.

    Outside
a woman lights incense—smoke rises—
                        she pats it on herself

and a girl collects petals
                by fingersful
beneath an airplane etched in marble.

The Son We Had

Pregnancy's first estrogen arouses you
the way Sunday morning bacon's aroma pulls me
from slumber, and wild with dormant hunger
you gorge on the hormonal surge inside
her left breast. Six weeks later
we miscarry, and with our fingers

find we carry you, a lump hard
at gestation north of the nipple.
On delivery the surgeon pronounces you
highly mitotic, healthy for your kind,
and we have you, our one and only,
a malignant baby bastard. I jumble
sounds from the word *disease*

and name you Sidney.
Something left of you inside
feels the kitchen growing hot
with radiation and rumors of richer tissue.
Oh Sidney, ungrateful son, you strike

out, leaving us no word.
You turn up in the liver,
a one-centimeter X ray ghost, and I give you
your own last name: Havoc.
Where have we failed, Sidney Havoc, that you
punish us with arrogance? What would it take

for you to know our grief, our love?
We send you the best in care
packages express, marked *chemo*:
Cytoxan
Adriamycin

5-Fluorouracil—5FU for short—*Fuck You*
Five Times, Sidney, it hurts that much.
If you could watch your mother's hair

falling over you, would you lose
your immunity to our sorrow?
Already your pimply sneer grows
smaller, receding in the crowd of normal
cells, until we no longer see you.
Yet however bereft and guilty of bad
parenthood these seven months, we know
better than to mourn
you, cocksure boy.

High-Dose Suite

1 The Bed

The bed was empty
when I walked into the room.
Where are you?
The stainless IV pole stood by, hooks
gleaming on the crosspiece.
Where are you?
The IV pole was bare as a winter tree,
the bed was empty, sheets pulled back,
and there you were in a red sweater
reading a mystery in the visitor's chair

waiting for me to take you home.
You followed me back down
the hallway of open doors, past the curled
gray forms inside, the grizzled morphined faces—
don't look, don't look—

followed me past the other end of Oncology,
past Admitting, to glass doors
that swung out, February's mist
a lotion to lungs
sucking the word *wife* into relief.

2 The Pole

She stood by you,
a stainless wet nurse with plastic udders,
suckling you, drip by drip, through tubes
that entered your chest near the place

where your left breast was given for a scar.
Cytoxan, Cisplatin, VP-16—
she measured these out, gave you her utmost
so that you might lie more helpless than a newborn
in your thirty-ninth year, your blood counts

all the way down to zero.
Ramrod-straight and conscientious, she attended
your vomiting and diarrhea, your five-day fever,
the burning knot in your lower intestine—
she saw to these as best she could, teats
swelling with antibiotics, platelets, morphine.
She is without fault, and give her credit

for this: unlike the doctors and other nurses,
unlike your friends and family and me—
all those who left you for the safety
of their own beds—for three whole weeks
she never left your side.

3 The Chair

The first day, I nestled into the green
padded home away from home, my corner
by the fifth floor window. Feet propped at the end
of your bed, elbows resting on wood arms,
I began to read you the folktale of a baldheaded
Japanese cat, and noticed, between pages,

the family member just across the hall
folding out his chair, lying down clothed
with a blanket, blinds darkening the room.
Pre-dose IV saline solution
put you in a drowse. Closing the book, I slid

down to join you in a nap, let the afternoon
take over the Space Needle, Olympic Mountains,
our island home between.

                           Hushed voices,
drifting shreds of sentences reeled me back,
eyes open to the sign—*No Entry*—
on the door across the hall, an orderly
and the family member talking—*body   morgue*

4 The Dream

It began to snow.
A flight of pigeons
spun incessant figure eights
while you spiked another fever, tethered
to your pole. I remembered the afternoon,

one day before admitting you here, we walked
on a beach carpeted with sand dollars,
live ones, dark gray, embedded
in slanting stacks. Turning one over,
I showed you the velvety spines
whirling slowly toward the center.
We walked on, the sky reddening,

and you told me your morning's dream:
We were in a barn, you,
and I, and our cat.
And horses, hundreds of horses.
When the cat started vomiting
blood, the horses all stampeded.

5 The Hallway

A-5 Oncology,
the voice at the other end of the phone,
connecting mine to yours:
draining the life out of me . . .
don't know if my body can take it . . .
just got to live through . . .

My footsteps took me past
the bald patient walking her IV pole,
the family member praying at the end
of a bed, past open doors, darkened
rooms, the eddies of suffering and morphine.
Each footstep, each breath contained
my heart, your life, each knock

on your blond closed door
contained my all—*oh please*
love lead us both out of here—
and you did.
                    Now, please, forgive
me the afternoon I walked
past your door, to the far window,
to see a white mountain in the east.

Trembling on my back in Emergency

towel balled and reddening in my hand,
I remember you smiling, calmer than I
with my arterial nick, an orderly
wheeling you in for amputation.
When I tried unscrewing a lamp fixture

the glass globe exploded in my hand.
Anything more than a handful, the adolescent
saying goes, is wasted. The breast
you gave—your left
our favorite—

vanished. A nurse soaps my finger's
base, red shoots against the wall,
wedding ring clatters in the stainless sink.
At a Christmas party, the baby you held,
as if your own, fingered your padded blouse,

chewed your red necklace.
A doctor arrives with blue thread,
explains a cut nerve at the second joint,
strings the moment like a bead.

Patient Belongings

I

Belongings: the short-sleeved blouse,
its paisley rayon desperate
to breathe light in your form;
the comb that hungers
for the pull of your hair;
the wristwatch, clicking in stir,

whose dream embraces your pulse.
Pathetic fallacy aside, how could
such things harbor a virtue
that stems from *pati*,
Latin, *to endure*? Endure
they do, with other items

you traded for a backless gown, personal
effects in a white plastic bag
with blue lettering.
Your liver endures the scalpel's maneuvers.
Prisoner of the Waiting
Room smothering me like a bag,

I endure the madness
of not knowing, the urge to lift
the fish tank, hurl it
through the window.
I fear the spot
of impatient cells.

2

Eleven years distant, your scar a highway
between belly button and breast bone,
eleven years free of those
cells—the biggest knock on wood
of our lives—and still you keep

the bag, nowadays to carry your mouse pad,
mouse and cables.
There it lies this winter evening,
empty, folded on the desk,

longings face up.
Your hand glides the mouse,
clicks, and another window shifts
the illumination of your face.
It could hardly contain my love, that bag,

even as I shudder back
to the leatherette chair, my heart
jumping each time a nurse in scrubs
passed through the swinging doors.

View, Teardown

San Diego, California

The chipped glass juicer, the Benny Goodman
78s, the armchair with its gouts of stuffing—
I step away from what remains inside
the house, take to the deck.
Tijuana anchors the horizon, Shelter Island's

docks hold yachts like bullets in a clip.
From the neighboring king palm tree,
birdsong rises above the roar
of Navy jets.
Oh mockingbird,

my mother's words come back, teaching
me your name in childhood: *That's a mocker.*
Blind in her last year, she heard you sing
incessantly from the same palm,
remarked, *It's a new bird, a mystery.*

The screen door slaps out front, car idles
in the red zone, my suitcase holding one thing
I did not consign to the shippers:
a four-leaf clover that fell out
of a book by a poet

named Teasdale.
My wife runs to tell me I'm late.
Mimus polyglottos, I finally remove
myself, so your song may bless
the swing of the wrecking ball.

3

Ramen-ya (Noodle Shop)

Five tables
in a hall-shaped room
                    lead to the kitchen
where he stands behind a stainless
                            steel counter

in a white shirt and white paper hat
facing the customers without expression
a ball of dough
resting like a cantaloupe in his hands.

He raises it over his head
brings it down to a deafening slam
then kneads it

lifts it again—
                slam—
begins a slow cadence
slamming the dough and massaging it

into a boa.
Doubling this over
he joins the boa's head to its tail
takes the middle with his other hand
                            and pulls

until his hands
            outstretched crosswise
hold two drugged snakes
                half again thinner
lengthening as he swings them back and forth.

Doubling them over
stretching and swinging again and again

he works a mitosis
        a geometric progression
of two to the fifth power: thirty-two

cream-colored vines
            strung between his hands.

He turns
and lowers them into a kettle of boiling water.

They arrive at your table in a wide
                    steaming bowl

topped with chicken or pork
                fish cake   shrimp.
Take your chopsticks and eat these first.

For the noodles
there is no other way but slurping loudly.
This cools them
        and signifies your gratitude.

Lift some from your bowl
hold them high for a moment—
                that's right—

now guide them to your mouth
suck in air and noodles
            at the same time:

a jet of steam
        blossoms in your lungs
the wish for longevity
            slides down your throat.

Finishing the noodles
tip the bowl to your lips
                    and drink the broth.

Now go out into the snowy
                    Tokyo night
your full belly radiating
                    the warmth of his hands.

Departure Mid-flight

Seattle-Glasgow

A flight attendant rushes a box—
Defibrillator—into First Class,
yanks the curtain shut. Somewhere

over the Arctic Circle, the pilot
dumps fuel to lighten us,
and we touch down at Iqaluit, Nunavut,

New Territories, the very edge
of dawn, squat buildings on tundra,
the palest of grays and browns.

Somewhere forward a stretcher is lifted,
a passenger journeys to a hospital.
It is said a man living

close to this place must hunt
three seals a week to feed
his family of seven. I finger the tiny

sterling box, my father's once,
which held the nitroglycerine
pills in his shirt pocket.

The plane refueled, its engines ease
into low roar, northern light
a shade stronger, stippling snow

and ice. My heart goes out
to all of us for whom Iqaluit
is not the middle of nowhere.

A single crow

lights near the end of a high
fir limb, hunches in the blowing rain.

There it rides, a shadow bobbing slowly
as the tree sways.
                    Within one glance

the crow has disappeared,
                    having seen what it saw,
and the branch tapers to gray.

How cold must this morning be,
                    how much colder,

now, this window, this table, this chair,
without the crow.

Checking In

I
You phone from St. Paul's
Rehab, Third and Nutmeg Street, dementia
floating you, a passenger in dock:
This ship's not as big
as the one that brought me from England

when I was thirteen, after my parents died.
You are the ship, and a physical therapist
pilots you between parallel bars—
like marine locks, they would raise you
and the hip replacing your fractured one.

2
Sighs the nurse, *I wish we knew*
what she was saying behind that mask.
When I pull it up, stretch
elastic straps by your nose and chin,
less than a minute passes before your lips

turn blue.
Both lungs
massively involved, pronounces
the doctor, *unable to swallow safely…*

ongoing downward spiral suggesting hospice.
You talk away.
I close your door.
Bedside, leaning toward your face, I hear

you say through the plastic,
Isn't someone going to bring me
something to eat? and later, *It's OK to cry,*

my son, and later, *Thank you all for helping
me to die.*

3

I lift the stethoscope from its hook
above your morphine, insert the ear pieces.
I part your purple shawl, place

the disc on your chest:
bubbles, sounding in slow procession,
a liquid form of the rattle with which
you fill the room's dry air.

Heard this way, your terminal breathing
reminds me of the whale's exhalations
in a CD I use to fall asleep.
I fold the tubing back over the hook,

hold your hand again, silently
take up your long-ago, lights-out rhyme:
Wynken, Blynken, and Nod one night...

4

Kitchen lights flash back on.
Beep! No messages. Click: returning power
surges into my low-tech answering machine,
erases, for good, your voice in clipped

tidings, hoarded several years for playback
when you would no longer be there to call.
Tips of bamboo that overnight snow
bowed to the ground
rise with morning rain, green flags

over moss and a slate stepping stone.
The refrigerator hums behind
all I can remember: *This is your old
mom, just checking in.*

All day taking up carpet

for the new owners in a house where an old man,
who must have smoked like a devil, died
four months ago, I cut it
down to rollable strips, shoulder
it to the driveway, fibers working
into the sweat on my arms and face. A job

is a job, and the last room is darkest,
its must filling my throat and lungs, coating
my tongue. Strip the place
they said, so I lift
Venetian blinds from their brackets, admitting
afternoon light, fuchsias outside
and the shadow of a star magnolia. Old man

without a name, did you
do nothing but smoke? Look on the stained
wall, a ghost where your colonial
mirror hung. Kneeling in the doorway I find
your trace, an L-shaped path in the carpet
leading around the foot of the bed
to your pillow on its eastern side. No bed,

no blinds, no nothing. Old man, were your slippers
brown, and leather, if you wore slippers? Did
boxsprings creak acceptance when you swung
your legs up and under the covers?
Did you notice a star, where the day
before there had been a flower bud? Did—
are you listening? Whisper something. Touch me

on the shoulder, I dare you.
To hear you padding toward sleep, to see
a match's flare, and in the flare

your hand. Instead, I leave you
all this carpet absorbed, a blessing
like sleep at the end of the day, a godless
prayer for both of us before
I lift the knife.

The Persistence of Memory

to Salvador Dalí, 1904—1989
"Take me, I am the drug;
take me, I am hallucinogenic!"

I Paris, 1931

You sit after dinner with a headache,
the table cluttered and Gala out to a movie,
train your eyes on ripe Camembert
softening over the edge of a plate,

lengthening under your gaze until it
almost touches the table.
The pressure builds. Time for bed.
First you rise and enter the studio,

turn the lamp on the unfinished canvas—
Port Lligat at twilight—
                    Mediterranean blue
darkening from the top of the sky

and the edge of still water along
a deserted beach. From the left
a dead olive tree extends a single branch.
Just as you reach for the lamp

you see two pocket watches
                    stretched out of compass,
one draped over the olive branch,
hanging like the tongue from a tired dog's mouth,

the other's hands still straight
but lost on a dial
          melting at five to six.

You mix oils and begin with the faces,
knowing where every hour will fall.

2 Port Lligat, Spain, June, 1975

Two fishermen talk quietly
mending their nets on the beach of soft watches.
Terraced olive trees
                    slope down to a white stucco house
whose roof bears two giant eggs
                                    standing on end.

My hand sweats around a plastic bag
that holds an abalone shell from California
as I watch the dark blue Cadillac below me,
Gala's knees through the smoked window,

your hand reaching over to pat them
when the engine starts and shifts into gear.
Leaping from the wall to the front of the car,
I flash the shell

like a stop sign at the chauffeur
then at the back seat: For you! For you!
You nod and your window slides down:
Thank you. Is very beautiful.
You speak the English? Yes.
You paint? No, I write.
You come see me and the Madame
tomorrow at seven. In the morning?
No, the evening.

The window slides up to encase you
and your car disappears in a cloud.
Dust settles on the empty plastic bag.

3 Copalis Beach, Washington, February 1989

Against a pewter sky
a juniper tree with one dead limb
thrown up in praise of its punishment by the wind
blasts the silhouette of a crutch. It becomes the crutch
you discovered in an attic when you were nine

the day you found your pet hedgehog
lying dead in grass.
Holding the bottom end of the crutch
you fit the crook around the bristled back
and gently turned it over to see a swarming
fist of worms in the belly. You ran

horrified to the mill stream
and held the crutch beneath the current,
then carried it to the linden orchard. A peasant girl
on a ladder cut blossom-covered branches,
tossing them down to a white sheet spread below her.
Intoxicated by the perfume

and the girl who reached with her pruning hook,
you placed the crutch on the blossom pile and waited.
After it was buried you pulled it out,
lifted it by the bottom end toward the girl,
gently fit the crook to the small of her back.
Dalí—*desire* in Catalan—

you tapped me playfully on the head
with the handle of your crutch-shaped cane
the evening I came to your home. Your eyelids
drawn back to reveal terrifying whites,
your moustache the horns of a Catalonian bull,
you said, *Now you will see the Gala
nude.* I followed you to your studio

and there she was,
full-length seen from behind,
radiating gold from a Mediterranean sunset,
the canvas almost covering one wall.
Thrusting binoculars into my hands

you said, *Here, you look through the wrong way,*
and the painting turned into the face of Lincoln.
Is fantastico, no?
Thirteen years later the painting
flanks your tomb. It isn't the painting
I remember most. It isn't the polar bear

umbrella stand, the candles drooping
upside down from candelabra, the wax
image of Christ on the Cross
you worked on, humming off-key, glasses
perched at the end of your nose. It isn't the time
you stopped to read my poem,
look at me and say, *Bravo, bravo*
or your comment, *You look like the Warhol
only much younger and thousand
times more beautiful.*

It isn't the sweep of your hand
as you drew a shooting star beside your name
and mine in the copy of your novel. It is one
translated sentence from that book:
*Inspiration is something one possesses
by the hard and bitter labor of every day.*
It is my sentence

to accept or deny every day,
a sentence that lasted me through the time
following your feigned kisses of farewell

on my cheeks that summer evening:
first, Gala's death

drawing in the life without desire.
Then your bed sheets in flames,
the wheelchair, Parkinson's disease
animating the watchmaker's hands,
oxygen tubes through your nose, your eyes

now terrified, eyes that once
saw an inkstand in a loaf of bread, Venus
de Milo as a chest of drawers—your vision
reminding me of the pearly
brilliance inside an abalone shell.
Here in a cabin on the bluff

at land's end, I turn on the lamp.
Sky darkens toward the ocean, leaving me
desire, blank sheets, a wrack of words,
my reflection in the window.

On Being Invited to Write My Last Poem on Earth

Hello, Father—*Aloha,*
hail and farewell, as the radio
announcer opened *Hawaii Calls,*
evenings when I was growing up.
The strains of "Sweet Leilani" carried you

back to your own youth, here
in my hand, garlanded in black and white,
Lei Day, 1936.
Leis crowd the chin of your mother
standing beside you on deck.

If each meeting is the first
meeting and the last meeting,
as the saying goes,
then this poem, Father,
is my first poem

and my last
poem to you, who died
before I took up the craft.
You grin your grin
of perfect teeth, your father

in the whites of a Navy Captain.
Father, I would tell you
of Marmot Pass in summer,
six thousand feet in the Olympic Range.
I would speak not of mountains

that surrounded me—Warrior,
Constance, Mystery, Deception—
but of the ant

that hurried across those peaks
on the outspread topo map

or of bees without number
plying a drift of lupine.
We measure our lives by what passes
before us: a photograph. That line
above my garden—the trace

flown by a chickadee just now,
linking cherry branch and rain gutter—
measures a lifetime.
The study of the low,
as K'ung-fu Tzu said,

penetrates the high.
For the first and the last
time, I grin back at you,
Father, your ship
departing Honolulu.

Hourglass

Sullivan's Island, South Carolina

On this beach where they landed—grains
of sand from Africa's west coast
in one historian's view, funneling
through Charleston, the pinched
neck of an hourglass—

sun burns the left
side of my face. Buckra
from a state where Douglas firs
rise through rain that has one hundred
names, I fail to find
a sign marking this as the place,

and currents diverted by a modern jetty
washed away the exact
location of the brick Pest House,
quarantine for human cargo.
Whelks and loggerhead turtles live
above bones of the spoiled
ones thrown overboard.

Each footstep takes on gravity.
If African Americans
have an Ellis Island on these dunes,
does battered Fort Sumter in the harbor
stand for the Statue of Liberty?
If I could grasp that, I could measure

the peculiar silence of the Atlantic
this morning. I could count the grains
of sand flowing into my palm
from this whelk shell, whose points
sharpen as they spiral outward.

(buckra: Gullah for white person.)

Oh Louisiana hog snout-deep

in an ordure of swamp water
surrounded by cypress trees with roots
surfacing like elbows and knees

attended by mosquitos and a mockingbird's
insistent song from a hidden branch
you stand still against withering heat

beneath shade that is no shade
and streamers of Spanish moss.
Your pink ear does not

twitch for the dragonfly lighting on it
your slitted eyes remain
immobile in their orbits

and you are beyond contentment
or serenity   beyond even bliss.
Your rounded shoulders

your bulk and symmetry
incarnate the Great Buddhas of Nara
and Kamakura

and I take this swamp over any lotus pond
this stench over clouds of incense.
All life is suffering.

Suffering is desire . . .
T-shirt soaked to my chest
dizzied by the whir of cicadas

I say to hell with the Four Noble Truths
The Eightfold Path
if only for these few moments

my heartache falls away before you
Buddha of the Bayou.

Properties of the Fence

Hammer back in its loop, nail belt
hung on a sawhorse, I gulp iced tea
you brought. Look, halfway through.
Posts and rails of the unfinished part
frame blackberry vines we hacked
far enough to string one property line,
drive stakes at eight-foot centers.

What does it stand for, this ache
the post hole digger slammed
into earth, lifted to my shoulders?
Each board, nailed, levels its claim—

mine—divides space the way a puff
of breath, mid-winter, frozen into a cloud,
separates one moment from the next.
Our side—now—and the other side—
then—plus all that abides: the fir root
blocking post hole three, the boulder
that made number eleven into a crater.

Sweat on the empty glass cools my temples.
I return to the stack of boards that await
Steller's jays, the darkening of September rain,
and blackberry vines come spring.

We cross the singe line

Mt. St. Helens
National Volcanic Monument

behind which the forest held, drive into gray
hemlock and fir thrown into their shadows
as if someone's forearm brushed them
down, reminding me
of the flattened bamboo grove we saw
black and white at a museum in Nagasaki.
At Viewpoint Ridge, trees all pointing
away from the blast suddenly stand

for cells, and I see red Adriamycin
rushing through your catheter in Oncology,
your hair falling in clumps by the wig stylist's
vinyl chair. Below the crater
a bedrock swath, sterile to the eye,
charts the landslide flushing Spirit Lake,
but through binoculars fireweed in pink
dots, firs poking through pumice and ash
summon the prospect—your seven months
chemo finished—of hairs emerging
from stunned follicles, your monthly blood
returning.

Port Townsend Valentine

1

From the lighthouse, agate in your hand
and in mine a round stone, gray with a white
band for wishing, we switchback up a bluff
to the old battery, where palms of lupine
cluster in Big Bertha's compass. Our concrete
woo's echo in the magazines and bunkers.

2

In the Shanghai Restaurant—white clapboard
former mess hall on Point Hudson—
we order on an outgoing tide, remember
the other Shanghai:
                              by the circular gate
of Yu Garden, won tons bubbled in a black
pan wide as a dragon's eye. Grinning, the vendor
offered them
          from a strainer on a bamboo pole.
Between Kung Pao Shrimp and Mu Shu Pork,
we read virtues of twelve animals on paper
placemats: two Horses are we, who should avoid
Rats in a zodiac without Cancer—fortune
enough for a day.

Laverne Under Mint

They dig by failing light, the man and woman
turning their shovels, catching the scent of mint.

Barbiturates, the vet explains, *three
injections. She may lose her bowels or urine.*

In a leap she's there, tabby purring on the dappled
quilt one Sunday morning as they lie in bed.

How deep? she asks. She must catch a Tucson flight.
Keep going. They dig, crows hawking in the high firs.

Back from Treatment with a foreleg shaved, bandage
securing the catheter, she purrs on the stainless table.

Under the quilt, their hands move between thighs.
The ancient cat climbs the woman's hip.

He angles the shovel blade outward, stabs
to square the sides of the hole. *Almost there.*

Lifted from the stainless table, she climbs to the man's
shoulder. He presses her neck to his ear—purring.

The man and woman shift, move together.
The cat crosses the quilt to the man's back.

By porch light they touch her neck. He curls
the tail around the paws. *Bury her in the towel?*

Nice kitty, the vet coos. Purring stops.
The man lays her on a towel on the stainless table.

Failing kidneys and all, purring, the cat
rides the man's back, the rolling musk of sex.

Why This Place

Conversation with a day hiker,
above Marmot Pass, Olympic Mountains

1

Striding, he catches us on our duffs, exclaims
What a spot! He distracts us from gouda,
smoked trout, Snyder's *Riprap*
and Cold Mountain Poems. To say nothing
of lines that peaks and ridges
cut into lowering light, Mount Mystery's
vertex acute enough to balance

a compass needle.
Twenty years—we astonish ourselves
replying to his question, *How long*
have you been camping here? Could it be
twenty Julys, lugging a gallon bag the last
mile, a thousand feet up from the spring,
packs fused with our backs?
Twenty Julys of alpine lupine unfurled.

2

As the full moon silvers my stream
of piss, I think on his parting words:
I myself like to stay on the move.
In his wake you and I have the blank book
of two more days open,
this plateau's altitude,

pearl jasmine tea.
The Big Dipper tilts toward the Strait.
I pull back the tent flap, crouch into the dark
promise of our lips, tongues

on the move across each other's bodies,
even with stakes that bursitis
drives into knees and hips.

Arakawa *O-bon*   (Summer Festival)

Dusk:
we sit on a bridge
         as the shore far below
fills with dancers
        to drums and flutes

for this week of the year
         they have gathered
from Tokyo and beyond
         to visit families
and the spirits of ancestors

to set oranges
    and cups of *sake*
beside candled portraits
        in alcove shrines.

Night begins to gather:
         red lights along the bank
hundreds of lantern boats

of rice paper and bamboo
         placed on the wide current
drift out in waves

thick as the mountain stars
         they mirror
each guiding a spirit back.

I try to follow one:
    it nudges against a boulder

drops into an eddy   swirls
        out among the others.

Tomorrow children will find them
            down river
moored among reeds
            and snags

but a few might bob
            even to Sagami Bay
before fibers open   swell
            and they sink under barges.

Boats my mother made
            from laurel leaves and twigs—

poems Bashō wrote
            sitting by a stream—haiku
                  he folded   floated—

launched and followed
            to a fork beyond the eye.

Lanterns drift below.
      Flower-fires burst in the sky
            lighting our faces.

Acknowledgments

My thanks to the editors of the following publications, where these poems first appeared, sometimes in earlier forms:

Bellevue Literary Review: "Patient Belongings"

Between the Lines: "A single crow"

Cider Press Review: "Why This Place"

Coachella Review: "View, Teardown"

Crab Creek Review: "All day taking up carpet," "Departure"

Crab Orchard Review: "Blacksmith," "Hourglass," "Pilothouse, the *Hoy Lass*," and "Mother's Day at Ninety-three"

Exhibition (Bainbridge Island Arts Council): "Anthropomorphic" and "Laverne Under Mint"

Hawaii Pacific Review: "Pages from a Wall Calendar"

Journal of the American Medical Association: "Back door towhee," "Figuring the Landscape," "Port Townsend Valentine," "Trembling on my back in Emergency," and "We cross the singe line"

Kyoto Journal: "*Thirty-six Views of Mt. Fuji*" and "Uses of Bamboo"

Many Mountains Moving: "Combination, 1968," "Morning," "On Being Invited to Write My Last Poem on Earth," and "Repository"

Nassau Review: "Eagle, Border Waters"

Northwest Review: "The Son We Had"

Passages North: "To transplant"

Permafrost: "Grace Below the Pass"

Poet Lore: "Departure Mid-flight" and "The Order of Things"

Portland Review: "Slow Starter" and "You call with a dead sea lion"

Seattle Arts Image (Seattle Arts Commission): "Miyajima, Boys Day"

Seattle Review: "Ramen-ya (Noodle Shop)"

Sow's Ear Poetry Review: "Love Notes"

Sycamore Review: "The Motorist's Prayer" and "*The Persistence of Memory*"

Upstream: "Pine Islands: A Letter to Bashō"

Wisconsin Review: "The Wedded Rocks"

The Written Arts (King County Arts Commission): "Kannon" and "Arakawa *O-bon* (Summer Festival)"

Some of these poems were published in a chapbook, *The Son We Had,* by Blue Begonia Press. Special thanks to Jim Bodeen.

"The Son We Had," "Trembling on my back in Emergency," and "We cross the singe line" were also included in the anthology *Under Our Skin: Literature of Breast Cancer* by Illuminati Press.

"Love Notes" and "View, Teardown" were also included in *The Inspired Poet,* a book of writing exercises by Susan Landgraf, published by Two Sylvias Press. Special thanks to Susan.

A brief excerpt from "Arakawa *O-bon* (Summer Festival)" appears in *Water Quilt,* a ceramic mural by Maggie Smith at the Nakata Pool on Bainbridge Island, Washington. Special thanks to Maggie.

"Epithalamium" was published as a limited edition broadside by Further Press. Special thanks to Elaine Smyth.

"Garden Without Figures" and "Urgent buzzing at my feet" were included in a chapbook, *The Girl Who Always Thought It Was Summer,* by *Raven Chronicles*. Special thanks to Kathleen Alcalá.

"Morning" was also included in *Spreading the Word: Editors on Poetry* by Bench Press. Special thanks to Debra Bokur.

"Oh Louisiana hog snout-deep" was included in the anthology *Animals as Teachers and Healers,* by NewSage Press and Ballantine Books.

"On Being Invited to Write My Last Poem on Earth" was set to music and performed as part of *Last Poem on Earth: A Jazz Requiem* in April of 2007. Special thanks to composer Paul Lewis, Bonnie Wallace, the singers and musicians, and the Bainbridge Island Arts and Humanities Council.

"Patient Belongings" received an honorable mention in the *Bellevue Literary Review's* 2009 Prize for Poetry, selected by Naomi Shihab Nye.

"The Son We Had" was also printed as a broadside by Clamshell Press. Special thanks to Don and Linda Emblen. This poem was also included in the anthology *Weathered Pages: The Poetry Pole* by Blue Begonia Press.

"Urgent buzzing at my feet" was first printed as a broadside by Floating Bridge Press.

"Uses of Bamboo" was also published as a limited edition chapbook by Further Press. This poem and "Back door towhee" were also printed as part of a series of bookmarks with artwork by Patty Rogers. Special thanks to Patty and to the Bainbridge Island Arts and Humanities Council.

"We cross the singe line" was also included in *Pontoon: An Anthology of Washington State Poets,* Volume One, by Floating Bridge Press.

"You call with a dead sea lion" was also included in *Pontoon: An Anthology of Washington State Poets,* Volume Two, by Floating Bridge Press.

I would like to thank Sam Hamill for help with "Kannon," "Oh Louisiana Hog Snout-deep," and "Pine Islands: A Letter to Bashō."

Special thanks to Akio Niino for opening my eyes to parts of Japan that I would not have otherwise seen.

Enduring gratitude for close conversation in poetry: Kim Anicker, Barbara Berger, Margi Berger, Tom Cullerton, John Davis, Eric DuVall, Gary Groves, Sharon Hashimoto, Kris Hotchkiss, Holly Hughes, Susan Landgraf, Bob McNamara, Kevin Miller, Arlene Naganawa, Nancy Rekow, Vern Rutsala, Derek Sheffield, John C. Smedley, Michael Spence, Dave Smyth, Elaine Smyth, Ann Spiers, David Stallings, Conrad Wesselhoeft, David Willson, Helene Willson, and Susan Willson.

Thank you, MoonPath Press editor Lana Hechtman Ayers, for your extraordinary gifts in shaping this group of poems, from its manuscript iterations to the book we hold in our hands.

About the Author

John Willson was born in Los Angeles and grew up in San Diego, where his love of nature sprang from many happy days by the ocean. Like his father, John excelled in high school track, running the fastest quarter-mile in San Diego his senior year. In 1968, when John was thirteen, his father died, one of the events that defined John as a poet and a person.

While attending Lewis and Clark College in Portland, OR, John met Kim Anicker, whom he married shortly after graduation. John's mentor in college, poet Vern Rutsala, served as a model for poetry as a life's calling and instilled in him an appreciation for poetry's grounding in everyday experience. In 1975, following an overseas study trip, John traveled to Spain and presented artist Salvador Dalí with an abalone shell. Dalí welcomed him into his home. The visit inspires John to this day.

John earned an MFA in Creative Writing from the University of California, Irvine, on a Regents' Fellowship. Shortly thereafter Kim and John moved to Japan, where they lived for a year and a half while teaching English to Japanese businessmen. Themes emerging in his poems from this period still abide in his work, revolving around man, nature, religion, technology, art, love, memory, and death.

After their return from Japan, John and Kim moved to another island, Bainbridge, on Puget Sound, WA. Here, John found a welcoming network of writers and served as the editor of the literary and visual arts publication of the community arts council. With a bias toward the visual element in his own work, John has collaborated with Bainbridge artists Gary Groves, Patty Rogers, Maggie Smith and others to produce resonant juxtapositions with their work and his, in forms including bookmarks, broadsides, a ceramic mural at a public pool, and a chapbook of his poems, *The Son We Had*, published by Blue Begonia Press.

John is employed by the Bainbridge Park District, for whom he has led a poetry writing workshop since 1992; and by Eagle Harbor Book Company, where he works as a bookseller and heads up the Staff Recommendations section.

Counting Theodore Roethke and Gary Snyder as primary influences, John considers himself a poet of nature whose work reflects lyric and narrative modes. His poems have been published widely in journals and in anthologies including *Pontoon: An Anthology of Washington State Poets; Animals as Teachers and Healers: True Stories and Reflections; Spreading the Word: Editors on Poetry;* and *Under Our Skin: Literature of Breast Cancer.*

John is a recipient of the Pushcart Prize and awards from the Academy of American Poets, the Artist Trust of Washington, and the King County Arts Commission. A two-time finalist in the National Poetry Series, he still lives with Kim on Bainbridge, where he has been designated an Island Treasure for outstanding contributions to arts in the community.

CPSIA information can be obtained
at www.ICGtesting.com
Printed in the USA
LVHW111727090320
649444LV00004B/883